AF598994

# VIDEO GAME TECHNOLOGY

BY AMY C. REA

childsworld.com

**Published by The Child's World®**
800-599-READ • www.childsworld.com



**Photography Credits**
Photographs ©: Shutterstock Images, cover, 1, 5, 12, 14, 21; Edward Condon/Wikimedia Commons, 6; Wikimedia Commons, 8, 10; Evan Amos/Wikimedia Commons, 9, 25 (top), 25 (top middle), 25 (bottom middle), 25 (bottom); John B Hewitt/Shutterstock Images, 13; Richard Drew/AP Images, 17; Matthieu Tuffet/Shutterstock Images, 18; Lucas Jackson/AP Images, 22; iStockphoto, 24; Diego Thomazini/Shutterstock Images, 26; Leonard Zhukovsky/Shutterstock Images, 28

**ISBN Information**
9781503869882 (Reinforced Library Binding)
9781503881358 (Portable Document Format)
9781503882669 (Online Multi-user eBook)
9781503883970 (Electronic Publication)

**LCCN** 2022951190

**Printed in the United States of America**

## ABOUT THE AUTHOR

Amy C. Rea is the author of several children's books. She also writes about travel and food. She lives in St. Anthony, Minnesota, with her husband and silly dog. Her first video game console was the Nintendo Entertainment System.

# CONTENTS

# FAST FACTS

- In 1940, Edward Condon displayed the Nimatron at the World's Fair in New York. This early video game is an ancestor of modern video game **consoles**.
- In 1972, the Magnavox Odyssey was released. It was the first home video game console sold to the public.
- In 1977, Atari released the Atari 2600. It used game **cartridges**, which meant gamers could play multiple games on one console.
- In 1985, Nintendo released the Nintendo Entertainment System (NES) in the United States.
- In 1995, Sony released the PlayStation 1 in the United States. This console used CDs instead of game cartridges.
- The PlayStation 2 was released in 2000. It used DVDs instead of CDs.
- In 2006, Nintendo released the Wii console. Wii controllers had motion sensors.
- In 2017, Epic Games released *Fortnite: Battle Royale.* Users could play together in a **virtual** world.

**New technology has improved the way video games look and sound. ► These developments have made video games more popular.**

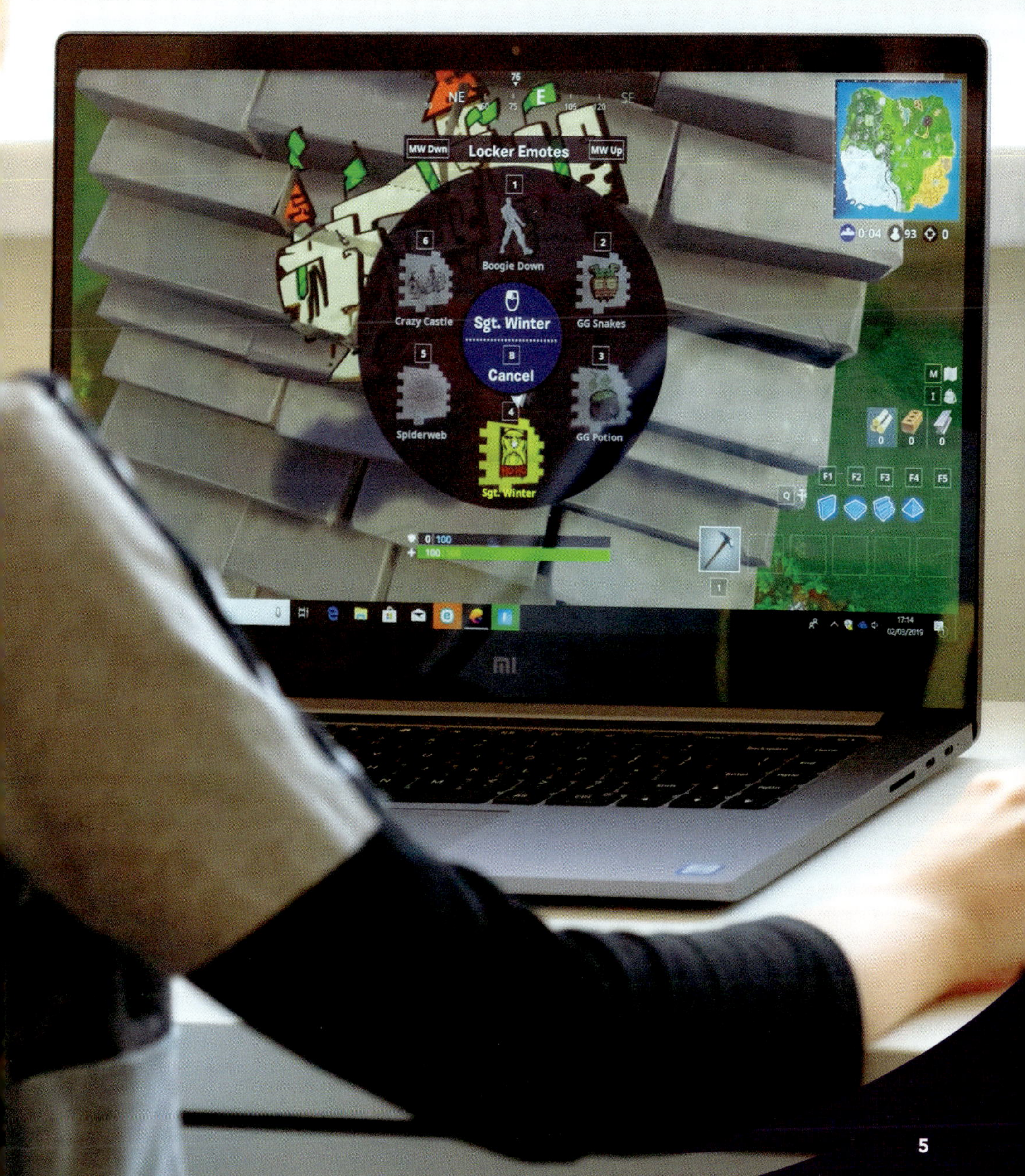
MW Dwn
Locker Emotes
MW Up
Boogie Down
Crazy Castle
GG Snakes
Sgt. Winter
Cancel
Spiderweb
GG Potion
Sgt. Winter

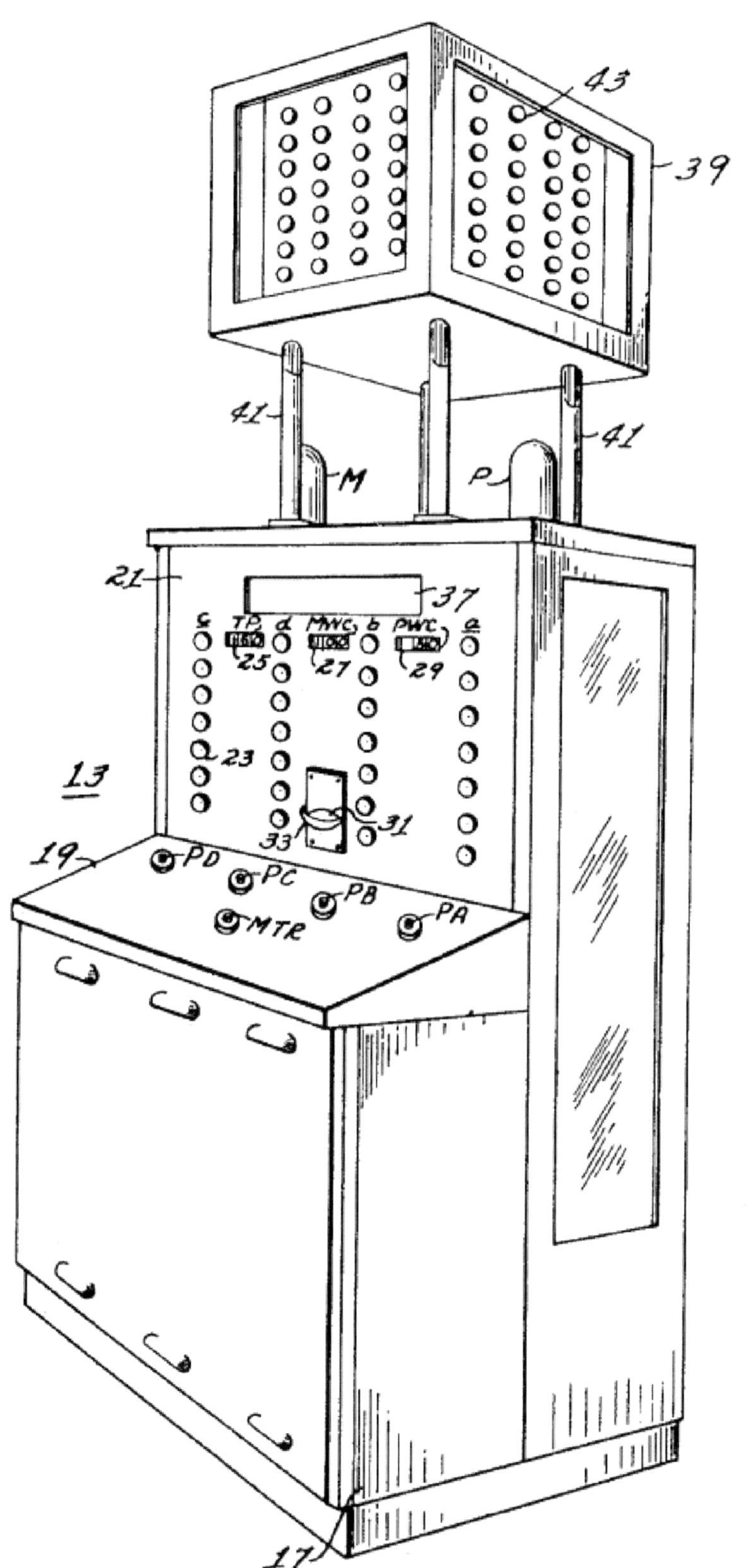
43
39
41
41
M
P
21
37
c
TP
d
MWC
b
PWC
a
25
27
29
23
13
31
33
19
PD
PC
PB
MTR
PA
17

CHAPTER ONE

# THE GAME OF NIM

Scientist Edward Condon stood near a tall machine with rows of lights and buttons. It was 1940. All around him, visitors to the New York World's Fair tried out new inventions. Condon watched as someone stepped up to the machine. She pressed a button and a few lights turned off. After a short pause, more lights went dark. The visitor was playing one of the very first video games: the Nimatron.

Condon invented the Nimatron for the World's Fair. Visitors could play the game of Nim against the machine. Nim was a popular game where two players tried to be the last to take stones from different piles. The Nimatron used lights instead of stones. Condon's machine played one side of the game. A human played the other.

**◄ The Nimatron had a large box on top of it with rows of lights on each side. These lights allowed visitors all around the Nimatron to watch the game being played.**

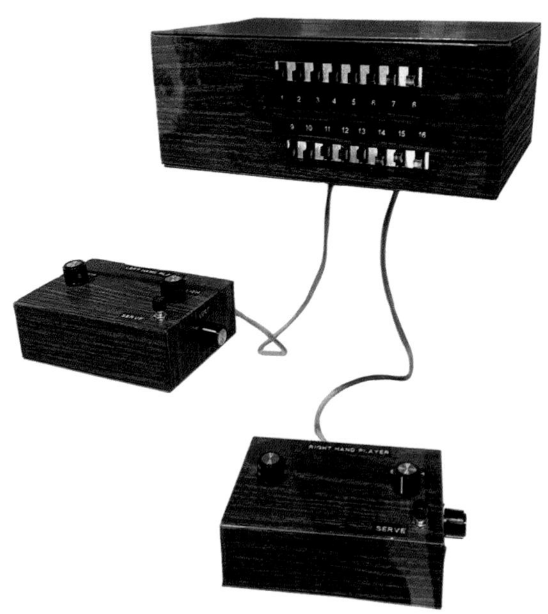

▲ **Replicas of the Brown Box have been shown in video game museums.**

It was the visitor's turn again. She pressed the button, and more lights turned off. Eventually, they all went dark. The Nimatron won. The visitor was one of many players to try this game. By the end of the World's Fair, around 50,000 people had played. The Nimatron won at least 90 percent of those games.

The Nimatron was the first ancestor of today's video game consoles. Condon invented it because his company wanted something exciting for people to see when they visited the World's Fair. It was successful. But Condon thought it could only be used at places like the World's Fair. The machine was 8 feet (2.4 m) tall. It would be impossible to carry places or use at home.

▲ **Players used three dials and one button on the Magnavox Odyssey controller to play games.**

It was not until 1967 that the first video game console was created. This one could be used at home. It was called the Brown Box. It could be connected to a TV set. There were two controllers. Two people could play games such as ping-pong and checkers against each other. The box had switches that could be set to play different games.

The Brown Box was only a **prototype**. In 1972, a company called Magnavox released a version of the Brown Box called the Magnavox Odyssey. It was the first video game console sold to the public.

Only around 300,000 consoles were sold between 1972 and 1975, when Magnavox stopped selling the Odyssey. It is still remembered as the first home gaming console. But not long after, new consoles and games were released. Each one would push video game technology further.

CHAPTER TWO

# ATARI AND *PONG*

It was Gus's birthday. The year was 1976. He and his family sat around the kitchen table. His family sang "Happy Birthday" to him. Gus couldn't stop looking at a big, wrapped package on the table. He bounced up and down in his chair. Gus hoped it was the *Pong* video game he wanted.

◄ **Some *Pong* video game consoles are displayed in museums today.**

When he ripped the paper off one side of the package, he saw large black lettering spelling *Pong* against a bright yellow background.

Gus was so excited that he cheered. His dad took the box to the TV in the living room. He connected the *Pong* game to the TV and turned them both on. Gus got ready to play a game of *Pong* with his dad. The console had two knobs to control the game. Gus and his dad sat close together so they could each use one of the knobs. This let them play against each other.

A white square began to slowly move across the black screen. *Pong* was like ping-pong or tennis. Gus and his dad used the knobs on the console to hit the square ball back and forth. The ball moved slowly at first. It sped up as they played. It was hard to move the knobs fast enough to keep up. Finally, Gus's dad missed the ball. Gus won. It was the best birthday ever.

The first home version of *Pong* was released in 1975 by a company called Atari. Atari had originally created *Pong* as an **arcade** game in 1972. Both versions of the game became very popular. *Pong* was similar to a game included on the Magnavox Odyssey. But the *Pong* console could only play one game.

▲ A ***Pong*** **player used the controller to move a rectangle on one side of the screen up and down. When the ball hit this rectangle, it bounced to the other side.**

In 1977, Atari released the Atari 2600 console. It was a home console with game cartridges. Players could plug in a new cartridge to play a different game. They could play many games on one console.

Atari went on to have many popular games. Some were home versions of arcade games. They included *Space Invaders*, *Asteroids*, and *Missile Command*. Other inventors took notice. Between 1972 and 1985, video games became more popular.

▲ **Game cartridges were loaded into the top of the Atari 2600 console.**

More than 15 other companies began working on their own video games and game systems. It was hard for Atari to compete. The video game console business was changing fast.

Nintendo
ENTERTAINMENT SYSTEM™
POWER
RESET
Nintendo®
SELECT START
B
A

CHAPTER THREE

# NINTENDO ARRIVES

It was a few weeks before Christmas in 1985. A Nintendo employee named Howard Lincoln was in New York City. He had been trying hard to get stores interested in the Nintendo Entertainment System (NES). He believed that this new console would be very popular if he could get stores to carry it. But he had worked long hours and hardly made any progress. As he walked down the street to visit another store, Lincoln came to a famous toy store called FAO Schwarz. He stopped in the street, his mouth hanging open in surprise. The FAO Schwarz window had a big display full of NES consoles. Lincoln thought that his hard work would finally pay off.

Video game companies were not making very much money in the early 1980s. There were too many game consoles for sale. Users thought many games were low-quality and terrible to play.

◄ **A version of the Nintendo Entertainment System was released in Japan in 1983, two years before the console was available in the United States.**

Atari had released a game based on the movie *E.T. the Extra-Terrestrial* in 1982. The game wasn't fun, and it was hard to play. It was so bad that many people started to think video games were simply a trend whose time had passed.

In 1985, the Japanese game company Nintendo released the NES in America. It was a much better console than what existed at that time. The NES had better **graphics** and sound. Nintendo had strict **requirements** for NES games. Game makers had to create high-quality games if they wanted their games to work on the NES.

But it was hard to get American stores to sell the NES. The stores were afraid they would lose money because video games had become unpopular. Minoru Arakawa was the head of Nintendo of America. He decided to offer the stores the chance to sell the NES at no risk to them. He told them they could return any unsold consoles to Nintendo for a refund. This was a big risk for Nintendo. But Arakawa believed that the NES would be a big hit if Nintendo could get stores to sell it.

He was right. The NES became very popular in the United States. The console was more advanced than other consoles at that time. Nintendo made several hit games, including *Super Mario Bros.* and *The Legend of Zelda*. These series are still popular today.

▲ ***Tetris* was one of the most popular games to play on the NES.**

Nintendo released other popular devices after the NES. In 1989, it released the first version of the Game Boy handheld console. Later, it would create the Nintendo DS and the Switch. Nintendo remains one of the top video game companies in the world.

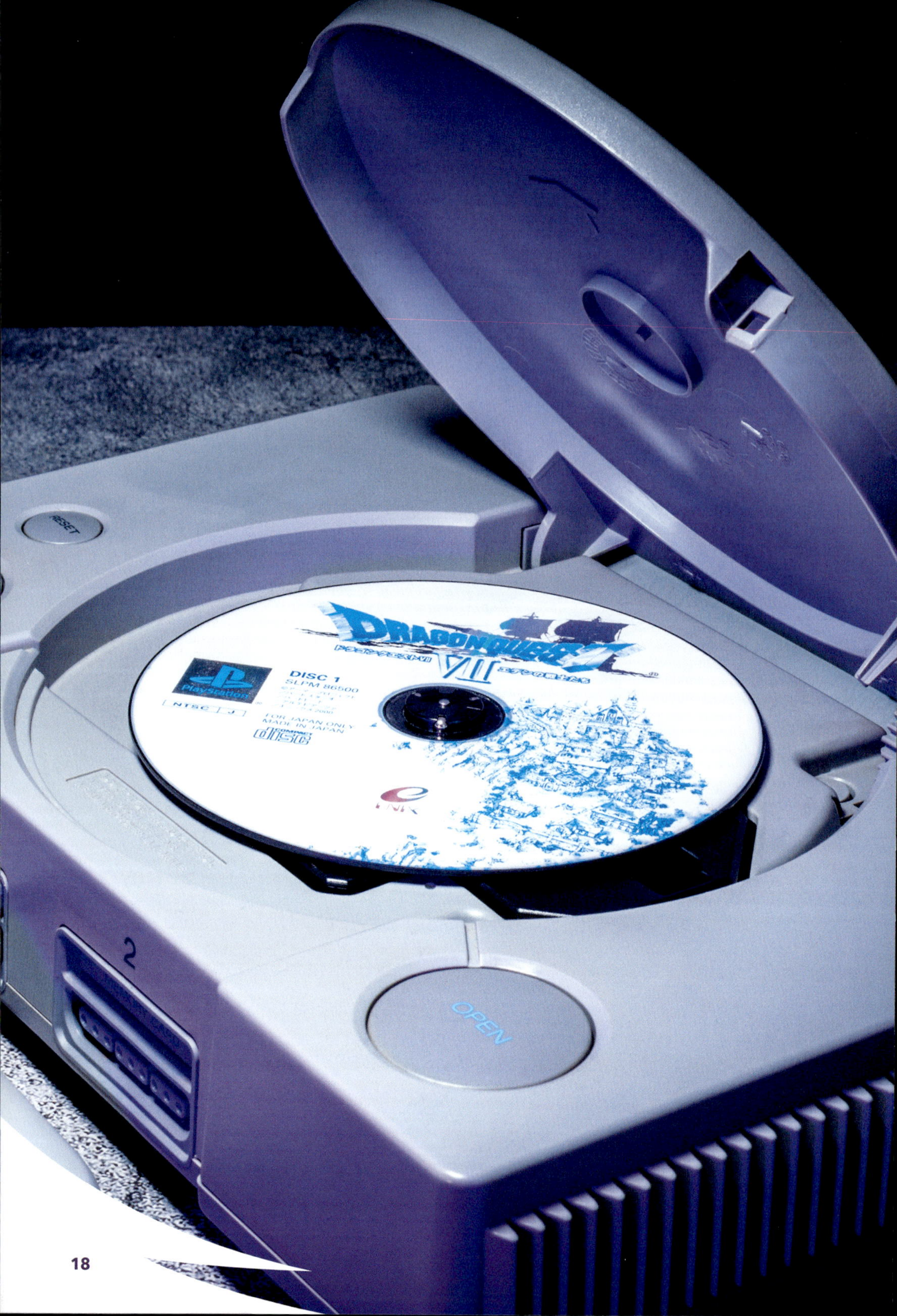
RESET
DRAGON QUEST
VII
DISC 1
SLPM 86500
PlayStation
NTSC J
FOR JAPAN ONLY
MADE IN JAPAN
ENIX
2
OPEN

CHAPTER FOUR

# SONY'S PLAYSTATION

Jessica had been saving her allowance and babysitting money for a long time. She wanted a new video game console. It was 1995, and her NES was old and out of date. All her friends talked about the new Sony game console called the PlayStation. It was supposed to be much better than the NES. At the electronics store, Jessica watched an employee playing the PlayStation 1 (PS1). She could hardly believe the graphics and sound. The characters and the setting were three-dimensional. The games looked more realistic than any she had played before.

The employee showed her how the PS1 used compact discs (CDs) rather than game cartridges. The PS1 was the only system that used CDs. The employee thought the PlayStation was going to be as big of a hit, if not bigger, than Nintendo's consoles.

**◄ The top of the PlayStation 1 opened for players to put in a game CD.**

Jessica decided to buy the PS1. She could hardly wait to get home and start playing.

Sony's launch of the PlayStation changed the video game industry. Nintendo and Sega had controlled the industry before the PS1 arrived. Sony had tried to work with Nintendo to develop a console. But the two companies did not agree. Nintendo was more focused on staying ahead of Sega, another company that made consoles. So Sony built the PS1 on its own.

Many different types of games could be played on the PS1. Sony made some games, but video game developers outside of the company made games for the PS1, too. Gamers could play everything on the PS1, including racing games, adventure games, and horror games. Nintendo and Sega could not easily compete. If people wanted to play PlayStation games, they needed a PlayStation console.

Sony released the PlayStation 2 (PS2) in 2000. It became the best-selling console ever. When Sony began developing the PS2, it used DVDs instead of CDs for its games. The PS2 was the first console that could play games on DVDs. People could also use the PS2 to watch movies on DVDs as well as play games.

The PlayStation competed against other new consoles that arrived. Nintendo's GameCube and Microsoft's Xbox were both released in 2001. But the PlayStation was still the most popular.

▲ **Video games in the *Final Fantasy* series were some of the most popular PlayStation 1 games.**

By 2005, the PS1 became the first console to ship more than 100 million units. Soon after, the PS2 hit this milestone faster than any console before it.

*CHAPTER FIVE*

# CHANGING THE CONTROLLER

A team of marketers were working at the Nintendo headquarters. It was 2006. They were trying to explain the company's latest game console: the Nintendo Wii. It had a new type of controller that looked nothing like the controllers available at that time. But it could do so many more things.

◄ **Reggie Fils-Aimé (left) and other Nintendo executives showed off the Wii in 2006. They played *Wii Sports* in front of a crowd to show how the remote worked.**

The Wii remote was **groundbreaking**. The trick was how to explain the controller to people who had never seen it before.

Reggie Fils-Aimé was Nintendo of America's president. He wanted to show how special this controller was. The key was its motion sensors. Players didn't just press buttons to move their characters. They waved the remote, and their characters moved the way the players did. Fils-Aimé wanted to create a commercial that would show all the ways players could use the controller. He wanted it to look easy and fun.

Finally, someone had an idea. A series of commercials would show two Japanese businessmen bringing the Wii to families. The businessmen drove to a home and rang the doorbell. They showed the family the Wii controller and said, "Wii would like to play." They visited many homes. Viewers saw the families and the businessmen playing all kinds of games on the Wii.

A father swung the Wii controller like a tennis racket. A mother used the controller to roll a bowling ball down the screen. A group of friends dueled in a sword-fighting game. Players punched, danced, and aimed. People of all ages appeared in the commercials. And they each held a Wii controller.

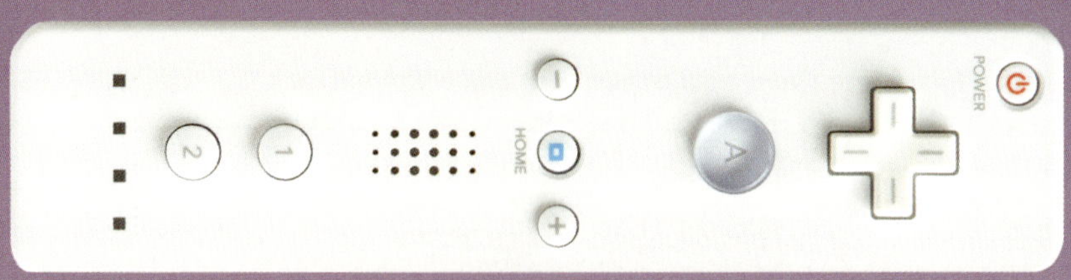


▲ **The Wii controller had a directional pad and other buttons in addition to its motion sensors.**

The Wii controller looked like a television remote. Earlier controllers were held with two hands. They were easiest to use for right-handed people. People could easily use either hand to play the Wii. But what truly made the Wii controller something new and exciting were the motion sensors. The Wii didn't rely on players pushing buttons or moving joysticks. Instead, as the player moved, the action on the screen changed. Players felt like they were inside the world of the game.

The Wii system was less expensive than its competitors when it launched in November 2006. Its ability to get players up and moving around made it popular for people of all ages. That included people who previously did not enjoy video games.

The Wii was very popular in the years after it was released. But the popularity did not last long. By late 2012, sales dropped. In 2013, Nintendo announced it would no longer produce the Wii. Instead, Nintendo focused on their other consoles, like the Wii U.

# VIDEO GAME CONTROLLER MILESTONES

The design of video game controllers has changed over time. Several milestones shaped the kinds of controllers available, even today.

**1985:** The NES controller was one of the first controllers to use a directional pad. It had up, down, left, and right arrows.

**1996:** The Nintendo 64 was one of the first controllers to include a joystick for the player's thumb.

**2005:** The Xbox 360 controller was the first controller to go wireless. It was also lighter than previous controllers.

**2017:** The Nintendo Switch introduced Joy-Cons. These controllers could be attached to the console for a portable gaming system or detached to play on a TV.

FORTNITE

CHAPTER SIX

# THE WORLD OF *FORTNITE*

It was August 2021. Callie had been waiting all day for this moment. She heard that her favorite singer, Ariana Grande, was holding a concert in the video game *Fortnite*. Finally, it was time. Callie logged on to the game. Callie's character went down a brightly painted slide. She slid through what looked like a bounce house and into the cockpit of a plane. Then she was in a black room lit by stars and giant bubbles in the sky. That was when Ariana Grande appeared. Callie couldn't help but give a scream of delight. This would be the best concert ever.

*Fortnite* was created by Epic Games. It came out in the summer of 2017. But it didn't become widely popular until Epic released a mode called *Fortnite: Battle Royale* later that year. Soon more than 10 million players had registered to play.

◀ **In *Fortnite: Battle Royale*, players fight against one another. They compete to be the last player standing.**

▲ ***Fortnite* brings players together in a virtual world. But video game tournaments bring players together in real life, too.**

The game came out for multiple platforms, including PlayStation, Xbox, Nintendo Switch, computers, and smartphones.

Epic Games continued to develop the *Fortnite* universe. Features were added so that users could watch virtual concerts, talk to other players, and explore educational parts of the game.

In 2021, *Fortnite* introduced Party Worlds. These are online places for players to meet each other and hang out. By 2022, more than 350 million players had logged on to *Fortnite*.

Video game technology has come a long way since Edward Condon's Nimatron. With *Pong* and the NES, early game companies began making consoles that could be played at home. The PlayStation's disc-based games pushed gaming technology further. The Wii changed controller design and got players up and moving. *Fortnite* brought more social activities to gaming. As technology continues to evolve, so will the video games of the future.

## THINK ABOUT IT

- Do you play video games? If so, have any of these milestones impacted the kinds of video games you play? How so?
- Do you think some people spend too much time playing video games? Explain why or why not.
- What kind of video games would you like to play in the future? How do you think new technology could make new kinds of games possible?

# GLOSSARY

**arcade (ar-KAYD):** An arcade is a place where many people can pay to play games, especially video games. *Pong* was first released as an arcade game.

**cartridges (KAR-trih-juz):** Cartridges are cases containing computer chips with the data for specific games. Video game cartridges are inserted into consoles like the NES to play games.

**consoles (KON-solz):** Consoles are boxes that hold the electronics used to play video games. The NES, PlayStation, and Xbox are all video game consoles.

**graphics (GRAFF-iks):** Graphics are the images produced by computers or video game consoles. The PlayStation had better graphics than the NES.

**groundbreaking (GROWND-brayk-ing):** Something that is groundbreaking is new and hasn't been seen before. The Wii controller was groundbreaking because of its motion sensors.

**prototype (PROH-tuh-type):** A prototype is the first version of something that is built to test an idea or a design. The Brown Box was only a prototype, so it was not sold to the public.

**requirements (ree-KWY-er-ments):** Requirements are things that are necessary. The NES had requirements for game makers that called for their games to be higher quality than previous video games.

**virtual (VUR-choo-uhl):** Virtual means something has been created using computer technology and is accessed using a computer. In *Fortnite*, players can meet in virtual worlds.

# SELECTED BIBLIOGRAPHY

Fils-Aimé, Reggie. *Disrupting the Game: From the Bronx to the Top of Nintendo*. New York, NY: Harper Collins, 2022.

"List of Home Consoles." *Game Medium*, n.d., gamemedium.com. Accessed 24 Jan. 2023.

Weiner, Charles, "Edward Condon-Session II." *American Institute of Physics*, 27 Apr. 1968, aip.org. Accessed 24 Jan. 2023.

# FIND OUT MORE

## BOOKS

Adamson, Heather. *Inventing the Video Game*. Parker, CO: The Child's World, 2016.

Green, Sara. *Sony*. Minneapolis, MN: Bellwether Media, 2017.

Shaw, Gina. *What Is Nintendo?* New York, NY: Penguin Random House, 2021.

## WEBSITES

Visit our website for links about video game technology: **childsworld.com/links**

*Note to Parents, Caregivers, Teachers, and Librarians: We routinely verify our Web links to make sure they are safe and active sites. So encourage your readers to check them out!*

# INDEX